OCT 1 2

What to Expect When You're Expecting Joeys:

A GUIDE FOR MARSUPIAL PARENTS
(and Curious Kids)

Bridget Heos

ILLUSTRATED BY **Stéphane Jorisch**

M MILLBROOK PRESS · MINNEAPOLIS

For my three joeys, Johnny, Richie, and J.J.
—B.H.

The author wishes to thank the following consultants for sharing their expertise:
Yolanda P. Cruz, Robert S. Danforth Professor of Biology, Oberlin College, Ohio;
Warren Pryor, Assistant Professor of Biology, University of Saint Francis, Indiana;
Marilyn B. Renfree, Laureate Professor, Director ARC Centre of Excellence for
Kangaroo Genomics, Ian Potter Chair of Zoology, University of Melbourne, Victoria

Millbrook Press
A division of Lerner Publishing Group, Inc.
241 First Avenue North
Minneapolis, MN 55401 U.S.A.

Website address: www.lernerbooks.com

Main body text set in Imperfect Regular 12/17. Typeface provided by T26.

Library of Congress Cataloging-in-Publication Data

Heos, Bridget.
    What to expect when you're expecting joeys : a guide for marsupial parents (and curious kids) /
    by Bridget Heos ; illustrated by Stéphane Jorisch.
        p.   cm.
      ISBN: 978-0-7613-5859-6 (lib. bdg. : alk. paper)
    1. Marsupials—Juvenile literature. 2. Marsupials—Infancy—Juvenile literature. I. Jorisch, Stéphane.
    II. Title.
    QL737.M3H46 2012
    599.2'139—dc22   2010051506

Manufactured in the United States of America
1 — BC — 7/15/11

CONGRATULATIONS, marsupial parent-to-be!

You have little ones on the way. You must be so excited! You're probably nervous too. Parenting is a big job. It's up to you to feed your babies, protect them, and keep them warm. Mamas, you'll do most of the parenting. In some cases, you daddies will help too. Sugar glider males, you'll guard, snuggle, and groom your own babies—and your nephews.

No matter what species you are, don't worry. You have instincts. They'll tell you how to be a mama or a daddy (or an uncle). If you're still curious, read on. Whether you're a possum or an opossum, a kangaroo or a wallaby, a koala or even a shrieking Tasmanian devil, we'll answer your questions here. You better read fast, though. Marsupials don't stay in the belly for long!

Q. Wait a second.
I thought I was
having a baby.
What's a marsupial?

A. It's what you are! As a marsupial, you give birth to very tiny babies that sometimes grow in a pouch. (You know, like kangaroos.) You mostly live in South America and Australia and its nearby islands. Virginia opossum, you are the only North American marsupial. Too bad people don't appreciate you more. They think of you as a giant rat. You're not even a rodent!

Basically, marsupials are a type of mammal. Mammals (including marsupials) have lived since the time of dinosaurs. Today mammals include grizzly bears, walruses, and marsupial moles. They all drink milk from their mothers as babies and have fur or hair on their bodies. (Yes, even walruses have traces of hair.)

While we're learning new words, you have a special name for your babies: joeys. If it's a boy, it stands for Joseph. If it's a girl, it's short for Josephine. Just kidding. Joey is just what your adorable babies are called. And to make matters even cuter, when your joeys are first born, they're called pinkies. Aww. Wook at da wittle pinkie!

Q. Will my—um, pinkies—look like me or their father?

A. That depends. Do either of you look like a slug with arms? No? Well, that's what your babies will look like! They'll be pink and furless. (That's why they're called pinkies.) Their little legs won't have feet yet. Their insides may even show through their thin skin.

Your babies are born very early. They'll spend only about 12 days in the belly if you're a southern brown bandicoot, Julia Creek dunnart, or Virginia opossum. You'll keep your baby in your belly for as many as 45 days if you're a Huon tree kangaroo. (And to think, human babies spend about 280 days in their mommies' tummies!)

When they're born, your babies are the tiniest mammals in the world. Honey possums, each of your babies is as small as a grain of rice! Red kangaroos, you are the biggest marsupials, but your pinkies are only the size of a jelly bean. That's okay, though. Your babies do most of their growing inside your pouch, also called marsupium. This is a pocket that covers your belly.

Q. Should I make the pouch with paper or cloth?

A. Neither! It grows on its own. Maybe it's already there! If you hop upright, like a kangaroo or a wallaby, your pouch will open to the sky. To you, it might look like a hole in your belly.

8

Koalas, you climb upright, but your pouch opens upside down. Don't worry that your baby will fall out. It's good at hanging on. And if need be, you can seal your pouch shut by tightening your pouch muscles.

Listen up, wombats, marsupial moles, and anyone else that spends time underground. Your pouch will open toward the rear. That way, it won't fill with dirt when you dig. Mama water opossum, you swim most of the day. But your baby hasn't had swim lessons. You'll seal your backward-facing pouch shut to keep out the water. (Daddy water opossum, you have a pouch too. But sorry, only mamas carry babies.)

Q. How many babies will I have?

A. That depends. If you're a Virginia opossum, you might give birth to more than twenty—and they'll all fit in a teaspoon! Sadly, only the first to attach to your thirteen teats (where they get milk) will live. This is nature's hard truth: having lots of babies at once usually means not all survive.

If you are a kangaroo, a wallaby, a koala, or a wombat, on the other hand, you'll likely give birth to just one. For months and months, it will be your pocket baby. Kangaroos, while one joey grows in your pouch, you might have another inside your body. Two joeys in the pouch would be too many. So your body presses the pause button—and the new baby stops growing. When your big joey hops out of the pouch, the little brother or sister starts growing again.

Q. How will my babies get into my pouch?

A. You might have heard stories about this. Maybe someone told you that your babies grow in your nose and you'll sneeze them into your pouch. Achoo! A pinkie! Nonsense. Your babies enter the world through your cloaca, an opening in your bottom. Then they make their way into your pouch all by themselves!

Even though they are so tiny, your babies have what they need for their trip to Pouchville: Strong forelimbs? Check. Sharp claws? Check. Giant nostrils? Check. Check.

this way to pouch

Keep going

You can make it

One Way

If you have a backward-facing pouch, your babies' trips will be short. But if your pouch opens toward the sky, your pinkie will face an uphill climb. Kangaroos, you can help by sitting on your tail and slouching. Make a path by licking your fur. Then your joey will follow the path straight up your belly. In a few minutes, it'll reach the pouch. Then it smells its way inside. (That's why it has those giant nostrils.)

Q. What if I don't have a pouch? Help! I've looked everywhere!

A. Stay calm. Many marsupials—such as common mouse opossums and short-tailed opossums—are pouchless. You can still carry your babies on your belly. By tightening special marsupial muscles, you'll pull them close to your body (sort of like sucking in your tummy).

But wait a second. Are you sure you don't have a pouch? Not all pouches look like kangaroo pockets, you know. Dunnarts, you have a circular pouch that opens in the middle. Antechinuses, your "pouch" is only a sunken area, like a giant belly button. As your youngsters get bigger, you'll need to arch your back so that they don't drag along the ground.

Don't let anybody tell you you're not a marsupial because you don't have a pouch—or because it isn't a pocket pouch. Your young are born tiny. Your milk and warm body help them grow. Plus, your ancestors were marsupials. These things make you a marsupial mama.

Q. What will my babies
do inside my pouch—
or on my belly—all day?

A. Drink milk! Constantly. They don't come up for air. Instead, they breathe through their noses. (Hurray, again, for big nostrils!) Once your pinkies start drinking, they won't stop for several weeks or months.

Your milk is just what your pinkies need. Thanks to lots and lots of it, their lungs will get stronger. Their ears will develop. Their hind legs will lengthen. Soon they will let go and take a break. Why? So your milk can change to another type of milk that helps them grow bigger.

Q. Will my babies grow too big for my pouch?

A. Yes! If you have several babies, they'll outgrow the pouch before they're old enough to walk—after just a couple of months. But you'll still be able to protect them. You'll leave them in a sneaky place like a burrow, a treetop, or a hollow log. Or you'll carry them on your back.

18

Honey possums, at night you'll leave your babies at home while you eat flower nectar and pollen. When you return, it's a honey possum love fest! Your babies will climb all over you and snuggle to keep warm. They'll poke their heads into your pouch to drink milk. Other times, you'll carry your joeys with you. You aren't the only marsupial to give piggyback rides. Opossums and koalas do too. But I know what you're thinking. Pigs don't give piggyback rides. It should be called a possumback ride!

Now, if you have just one baby, you'll keep it in the pouch for longer. Let's say you're a red kangaroo. After about five months, your joey pokes its head out. It sees you chomping grass. It thinks, "A snack that's not milk? How thrilling!" Soon it nibbles some grass from the safety of your pouch. One day it might lean over too far and fall out. Or get curious and hop out. Or you might tip your joey out. However it happens, it's called your joey's second birth. Say, "Happy second birth-day, joey!"

Q. Will I miss my baby?

A. Probably not. Because in two minutes, little red will dive back in—headfirst. The world is big. The world doesn't have free milk. So your joey will still come back to the pouch.

You'll sometimes want it to be in the pouch too. If you sense danger, such as a dingo on the prowl, you'll stamp your feet to tell joey to climb in. Then you can make your getaway together.

When your joey is about eight months old, you'll think it's getting too big for the pouch. Will it jump in and out forever? No. Say, "You're a big roo now. You need to hop on your own two feet. No more pouchy time." You can't talk, so say this by shutting your pouch until joey gets tired of trying. The next day, a new pinkie will be born!

Q. Where will my older joey go when it moves out of my pouch?

A. Nowhere—yet. Whether you gave birth to just one baby or a large litter, they'll stick around. While they can no longer climb inside the pouch, they still poke their heads in for milk. They're also beginning to eat what you eat.

If you're a koala, your baby will munch on eucalyptus leaves. This food is low in nutrition and doesn't provide you or your cub with much energy. So you save energy by sleeping twenty hours a day, hugging each other for warmth, and having small brains. You aren't the sharpest eucalyptus branches on the tree! But you are the cutest.

Tasmanian devils, your babies will fight over their food. They'll screech and bite and play tug-of-war. Be sure to encourage this behavior. It prepares them for adulthood. As grown-ups, they'll feast as a group on dead animals. These "dinner parties" aren't pleasant! If you want scraps, you've got to be scrappy. Your babies learn to fight for their food by practicing with their brothers and sisters!

Whatever kind of marsupial you are, your youngsters will eventually stop drinking milk. This can happen when your joey is just a few months old—or a little over a year. But it always means the same thing: your joeys are growing up.

Q. What happens next?

A. Your babies (which are not babies anymore) will soon leave your side. Don't worry. You won't be lonely. If you live in a group, some of your children will stay nearby. Kangaroos, your group is called a mob. Girl kangaroos often join their mothers in the mob. Boys, on the other hand, leave. They get big and strong and box with each other over girl kangaroos. How roo-mantic.

26

If you are an animal that lives alone—and most marsupials do—you and your babies will say good-bye. But you won't be lonely, either. For you, parting is natural. Let's say you're a Tammar wallaby. This is a kangaroo cousin just 6 inches (15 centimeters) long (or 18 inches [46 cm], if you count your ginormous tail). You have a baby every year from about the age of one to thirteen. While you're having babies, your grown-up babies will have babies. Then their babies will have babies. If you stayed together, there would be mothers and babies everywhere. Instead, you fly solo.

You might see your daughter in the evening while you are feeding. (She'll be hard to miss with that tail.) You might both have pinkies growing inside your pouch. You won't offer to babysit, though. You'll only care for your own joey. Your daughter will only care for her joey. And that joey, when it grows up, will only care for its joey.

But that is enough to keep the family going. Pinkies will continue to be born and make their way into pouches. They'll look funny at first but will grow to be whatever they are meant to be. Just as your joeys did. Just as you did. And just as marsupials have done since the age of dinosaurs.

The End . . . and the Beginning.

GLOSSARY

burrow: a tunnel that an animal digs

cloaca: the opening in the bottom through which marsupials deliver babies

cub: a baby bear, wolf, large cat, or whale; a baby koala. A long time ago, people started calling koalas "koala bears." They named koala joeys "cubs." Koalas aren't bears. They're marsupials. But they do kind of look like bears (teddy bears, that is).

forelimbs: the front legs of animals. For marsupials that stand on their hind legs, these are also known as arms. You know what an arm is, right?

instincts: built-in knowledge or behaviors

joey: a nickname for a boy named Joseph; a nickname for a girl named Josephine; a baby marsupial, which is short for "hi-I'm-a-young-marsupial-but-you-can-call-me-joey"

litter: a group of babies born to the same mother at the same time

mammal: a class of warm-blooded animals in which mothers feed their young milk from mammary glands

marsupium (pl. marsupia): a pouch in which some marsupials carry their young

mob: a group of kangaroos that live together as a social group

nectar: the juice of a flower; to honey possums, a midnight snack

pinkie: a very young joey; a very small finger

pollen: fine grains produced by seed plants, which help the plants reproduce; to honey possums, more moonlight treats

second birth: the point in time when baby marsupials exit the pouch

teat: the part of an animal from which babies get their milk

SELECTED BIBLIOGRAPHY

Animal Diversity website. 1999. http://animaldiversity.ummz.umich .edu/ (October 29, 2009).

Armati, Patricia J., Chris R. Dickman, and Ian D. Hume. *Marsupials*. Cambridge: Cambridge University Press, 2006.

Dickman, Christopher. *A Fragile Balance: The Extraordinary Story of Australian Marsupials*. Illustrated by Rosemary Woodford Ganf. Chicago: University of Chicago Press, 2007.

Nowak, Ronald M. *Walker's Marsupials of the World*. Baltimore: Johns Hopkins University Press, 2005.

Tyndale-Biscoe, Hugh. *Life of Marsupials*. Collingwood, Australia: Csiro Publishing, 2005.

Tyndale-Biscoe, Hugh, and Marilyn Renfree. *Reproductive Physiology of Marsupials*. Cambridge: Cambridge University Press, 1987.

FURTHER READING AND WEBSITES

BOOKS

Bishop, Nic. *Marsupials.* New York: Scholastic Nonfiction, 2009.
See amazing photos and learn more about many different marsupials.

Collard, Sneed B. *Pocket Babies and other Amazing Marsupials.* Minneapolis: Millbrook Press, 2007.
Discover more detailed information about marsupial babies—both those who live in pockets and those who don't.

Eckart, Edana. *Koala.* Welcome Books series. New York: Children's Press, 2005.
Koalas aren't bears. They're marsupials. Find out more about koalas in this book.

French, Jackie, and Bruce Whatley. *How to Scratch a Wombat: Where to Find It . . . What to Feed It . . . Why It Sleeps All Day.* New York: Clarion Books, 2009.
What would it be like to have wombats living in your backyard? This author found that out firsthand.

Markle, Sandra. *Tasmanian Devils.* Minneapolis: Lerner Publications Company, 2006.
Tasmanian devils have gotten a bad rap. Read this book to learn the truth about these cuddly creatures. (Okay, maybe "cuddly" is a slight exaggeration.)

Swan, Erin Pembrey. *Meat-Eating Marsupials.* New York: Franklin Watts, 2002.
Most marsupials don't eat meat, but this book focuses on those that do.

WEBSITES

Australian Museum
http://www.australianmuseum.net.au
This museum is dedicated to culture and nature in Australia, including marsupials.

The Marsupial Society of Australia
http://www.marsupialsociety.org
This society supports and guides those who care for rescued marsupials. Their website also has coloring pages and activities for kids.

Opossum Society of the United States
http://www.opossumsocietyus.org/
This society educates people about North America's only marsupial, the opossum. Their website includes a word find and a coloring page.

RooGully's Channel
http://www.youtube.com/user/RooGully
This YouTube channel offers a series of documentary videos about a wildlife sanctuary that cares for sick, injured, and orphaned kangaroos.

Tasmanian Devil Conservation Park
http://www.tasmaniandevilpark.com/
The website of this wildlife sanctuary for Tasmanian devils includes photos and news about these meat-eating marsupials.

 LERNER SOURCE Expand learning beyond the printed book. Download free, complementary educational resources for this book from our website, www.lerneresource.com

ABOUT THE AUTHOR

Bridget Heos is also the author of *What to Expect When You're Expecting Larvae: A Guide for Insect Parents (and Curious Kids)*. She has written more than twenty nonfiction books for children of all ages. She lives in Kansas City, Missouri, with her husband and three sons. Although she has no known baby marsupials living at her house, she does have a nephew named Joey Bag-a-Donuts. Visit Bridget on the Web at www.authorbridgetheos.com.

ABOUT THE ILLUSTRATOR

Stéphane Jorisch is a full-time illustrator who has received several prestigious Canadian honors for his work, including a 1993 Governor General's Award; nominations for Governor General's Awards in 1995, 1997, and 1998; and nominations for the 1997 and 1999 Mr. Christie Book Awards. Jorisch works in a huge loft in Montreal, Quebec, with several other designers and illustrators. He believes that curiosity and a keen sense of observation are most important for an aspiring writer or artist.